This bool
is to com

that future glory breaks in to this present
world. Thank you, Dr. Thomas, for offering
biblical wisdom and insight into what living the
Christian life is all about.

Stephen J. Nichols
Author of *R. C. Sproul: A Life*
President, Reformation Bible College, CAO
Ligonier Ministries, Sanford, Florida

'Our citizenship is in heaven, and from it we
await a Savior, the Lord Jesus Christ, who will
transform our lowly body to be like his glorious
body' (Phil. 3:20-21). 'We know that when he
appears we shall be like him, because we shall
see him as he is' (1 John 3:2). This astonishing
prospect and promised hope is part of the
gospel fuel that powers the Christian life. Derek
Thomas faithfully and beautifully expounds it
in this little book. Part of Christian discipleship
is getting this hope down into your heart until
you really believe it, and it begins to change
your longings and your living. Dr. Thomas, as
a sympathetic shepherd, will guide you in the
truth of glorification to that end.

Ligon Duncan
Chancellor and CEO,
Reformed Theological Seminary

A bright, thoughtful, engaging and much needed introduction to the wonder and power of God's presence made known.

Jonny Dyer
Associate Rector, All Souls Langham Place, London

TRACK
DOCTRINE

A STUDENT'S GUIDE TO

GLORIFICATION

DEREK W. H.
THOMAS

SERIES EDITED BY
JOHN PERRITT

CHRISTIAN
FOCUS

rym

Copyright © Derek W. H. Thomas 2021

paperback ISBN 978-1-5271-0696-3
ebook ISBN 978-1-5271-0783-0

10 9 8 7 6 5 4 3 2 1

First published in 2021
by
Christian Focus Publications Ltd,
Geanies House, Fearn, Ross-shire,
IV20 1TW, Great Britain

www.christianfocus.com

with

Reformed Youth Ministries,
1445 Rio Road East
Suite 201D
Charlottesville,
Virginia, 22911

Cover by MOOSE77

Printed by Page Bros, Norwich

CONTENTS

Leslie and Barbara Holmes
'there is a friend who sticks closer than a
brother.' (Prov. 18:24)

Series Introduction

Christianity is a religion of words, because our God is a God of words. He created through words, calls Himself the Living Word, and wrote a book (filled with words) to communicate to His children. In light of this, pastors and parents should take great efforts to train the next generation to be readers. *Track* is a series designed to do exactly that.

Written for students, the *Track* series addresses a host of topics in three primary areas: Doctrine, Culture, and the Christian Life. *Track's* booklets are theologically rich, yet accessible. They seek to engage and challenge the student without dumbing things down.

One definition of a track reads: *a way that has been formed by someone else's footsteps.* The goal of the *Track* series is to point us to that 'someone else'—Jesus Christ. The One who forged a track to guide His followers. While we cannot follow this track perfectly, by His grace and Spirit He calls us to strive to stay on the path. It is our prayer that this series of books would help guide Christ's Church until He returns.

In His Service,

John Perritt
RYM's Director of Resources
Series Editor

Introduction

⎯⎯⎯

Why a book about glorification? And why should you care about this topic? More to the point, what on earth is glorification? I put it that way because it is something that happens on earth, in this life, in the experience of every Christian. As we shall see, the apostle Paul tells us in the magnificent eighth chapter of Romans that there is a sense in which we have been glorified *already*. True, glorification is about what happens when we go to heaven and when we experience bodily resurrection at the return of Jesus Christ. That's in the future. But we are given a little taste of it right here and now.

In the Bible, the word *glory* is translated in over twenty different words—twelve in Hebrew and eight in Greek. There are over 370 verses in the Bible that contain the word *glory*. Sometimes its meaning is akin to the idea of praise. On other occasions, the idea in view would be similar to honor or majesty. The most common Hebrew word for glory (*kâbôd*) as well as the Greek (*doxa*) have as their root meaning the idea of heaviness or weightiness.

I am someone who was a teenager in the 60s and can recall how popular it was to say 'that's heavy, man!', meaning that the matter was deep and significant. If you've ever seen the 80's film, *Back to the Future*, you may recall Marty saying, 'That's heavy, Doc'. This idea of *glory* seems to be something popular culture is more aware of than we think. Maybe we could say that you are much more aware of this notion than you realize.

Whenever the word is used of God, it conveys the idea of majesty and greatness. God is great and awesome, and Christians desire to tell Him so and to worship Him in a manner that exalts Him.

But glory is also an aspect of redeemed humanity. There is something awesome about *us*, too. To cite Hamlet, 'what a piece of work is a man!' In a world that increasingly devalues humanity, where far too many have little respect for themselves or others, and more pertinently, where women and men experience the sadness and anxiety that accompanies a sense of worthlessness, we need to know about the glory that God bestows on us. Have you ever realized that you are a glorious being? Even when your friends ditch you. Even when you mess up for the umpteenth time.

ALL-AROUND GLORY

Furthermore, glory is a term that is used in Scripture for natural objects such as the brightness of heavenly bodies (Acts 22:11; 1 Cor. 15:41), the fruitfulness of a forest (Isa. 35:2; 60:13), the sound of a horse's snorting (Job 39:20), or the beauty of expensive clothing (Luke 7:25). If we have eyes to see it properly, the world, even in its fallen state, is majestically beautiful. The universe is a thing of glory. But, as they say, 'you ain't seen nothing yet!' There is even more glory to come.

The glory of God is seen in creation and redemption. But it is most evident in the incarnate Jesus. Describing the incarnation of the Son of God, John summarized it this way: 'And the Word became flesh, and dwelt among us, and we saw His glory, glory as of the only begotten from the Father, full of grace and truth' (John 1:14). He is the *radiance* of God's glory (Heb. 1:3). And Christians are going to be made like Him in His glory; we are right now being conformed to His image (Rom. 8:29). What a wonderful thing it is to be a Christian!

This book will examine how this divine glory is reflected in redeemed humanity. We will explore how humanity lost this glory at the Fall, and how it is restored in part at the time of new birth (salvation). We will also take some time to look ahead and ask how this glory will manifest itself in heaven and beyond that, in the new heaven and new earth which is our destiny in Christ. Of course, given the scope of these short student guides, we cannot possibly explore these ideas as fully as possible, and we will have to be content with a summary. Summaries are often as helpful as intense, microcosmic studies of topics. Sometimes it is fun to look down from 36,000 feet, as we do when we fly somewhere and view the entire terrain below. That's a bit like what we will do in this study. I hope it will give you a renewed sense of the glory of God and the glory He intends for every Christian.

So, what is glory? Let's go back to the beginning and find out.

1. Glory Begun

How often do you look in the mirror? Most of us use mirrors all the time. Getting ready in the morning and backing out of the driveway are fairly common ways to make use of a mirror. When we look in a mirror, we see our reflection. It's not actually us in the mirror, but it is a true reflection of who we are. Well, there's a sense in which you and I reflect our Creator.

Humanity was created to reflect something of the glory of God. In a crucially important statement, the first chapter of the Bible tells us that Adam and Eve were created to reflect God Himself:

> *So God created man in his own image,*
> *in the image of God he created him;*
> *male and female he created them*
> *(Gen. 1:27).*

Moses repeats this idea later in Genesis using the word 'likeness': 'When God created man, he made him in the likeness of God' (Gen. 5:1). And two verses later, we read that Adam had a son 'in his own likeness, after his image, and named him Seth' (Gen. 5:3). Among other things, Moses is saying that Seth looked like his father. In a similar way, Moses is saying that Adam and Eve looked a little bit like God! More especially, Adam and Eve reflected incarnate Jesus, who is the supreme glory of God (Heb. 1:3). All creation 'declares the glory of God' (Ps. 19:1), but only humans are made in God's image.

That last sentence needs a little unpacking lest we take it in entirely the wrong way. We are not to think that Adam and Eve were divine in some way. No, they were entirely human. Nor should we think that God has a body, with arms and legs, eyes and ears. Despite the fact that the Bible uses language suggesting that God 'walked in the Garden in the cool of the day' (Gen. 3:8), we are not to think of that in the literal sense. As Jesus reminded the woman of Samaria, 'God is spirit' (John 4:24).

Genesis 1:27 teaches us that there are qualities and attributes of Adam and Eve that reflect God's own nature and being. Precisely how does humanity (before the Fall) reflect the image of God? Church history has really struggled to answer this question!

HUMANS ARE THE APEX OF GOD'S CREATION

Part of the mystery involves the fact that divine image-bearing is something that is only said of human beings, *not animals, or birds, or fish.* Theologians have therefore suggested that what is unique to human beings is the fact that they 'have a soul.'

The King James Version of the Bible, for example, translates Genesis 2:7 this way: 'And the Lord God formed man of the dust of the ground, and breathed into his nostrils the breath of life; and man became a living soul.' The term soul is only used of human beings. But this entirely misses the fact that the Hebrew word translated as 'soul' is also translated as 'living' when it describes fish, cattle, creeping things and birds (Gen. 1:20, 24, 30). Adam and Eve's soulishness was something they had in common with other creatures.[1] All of them had

---

1   By the way, we shouldn't say that humans *have* souls (more of a Greek idea than a biblical one). Rather, we should say that humans *are* souls.

life. The ESV is therefore correct to simply say in Genesis 2:7, 'man became a living creature.'

Others have turned to concepts like rational thought or deep personal relationships, but these, too, are evident in other creatures and don't fully explain what makes humans unique. Again, some have suggested that only humans are self-aware. Quite how this conclusion is derived is unclear, but when elephants have a white spot painted at a spot between their eyes and they see their reflection in the water, they will attempt to remove it, thereby demonstrating that they too are very much self-aware.

A better answer is to point out the connection of the words, 'in our image,' with what immediately follows: 'Be fruitful and multiply and fill the earth and subdue it, and have dominion over the fish of the sea and over the birds of the heavens and over every living thing that moves on the earth' (Gen. 1:28). Humanity is asked to share in God's rule over the universe in a manner quite distinct from the rest of the creatures. God and humans are partners in this enterprise. This view stands in marked contrast to that peddled in our culture today where all creatures are equal.

THE SANCTITY OF HUMAN LIFE

All of this has huge ramifications, not least to the sanctity of life. Interesting that murdering one made in the image of God is a capital offense:

Whoever sheds the blood of man,
  by man shall his blood be shed,
for God made man in his own image
(Gen. 9:6).

Whatever your views on capital punishment in the twenty-first century, passages like this show how seriously God values the life of each human being. Murder is horrific not just because it ends someone's life, but because it destroys something that carries the image of God Himself.

We take it for granted that most people know that murder is morally wrong. But what do we base that judgement on, if not the knowledge that humans are set apart by God? Peter Singer of Princeton University, a contemporary and influential ethicist, writes:

Whatever the future holds, it is likely to prove impossible to restore in full the sanctity-of-life view. The philosophical foundations of this view have been knocked asunder. We can no longer base our ethics on the idea that human beings are a special form of creation made in the image of God, singled out from all other animals, and alone possessing an immortal soul. Our better understanding of our own nature has bridged the gulf that was once thought to lie between ourselves and other species, so why should we believe that the mere fact that a being is a member of the species Homo Sapiens endows its life with some unique, almost infinite value?[2]

If we don't understand that we are made in the image of God, much of our Western ethical system crumbles. God wants us to know that there is something wonderfully unique about the human race. Humanity is God's supreme creation. It is a theme that caused the psalmist to say:

What is man that you are mindful of him,
and the son of man that you care for him?
*   Yet you have made him a little lower than*
the heavenly beings

---

2   Peter Singer, 'Sanctity of Life or Quality of Life?' *Pediatrics* 72, no.1 (July 1983): 128-129. Cited by John C. Lennox, *Seven Days That Divide the World: The Beginnings According to Genesis and Science* (Zondervan, Grand Rapids, MI: 2011), 68.

and crowned him with glory and honor.
You have given him dominion over the
works of your hands;
you have put all things under his feet,
all sheep and oxen,
and also the beasts of the field,
the birds of the heavens, and the fish of
the sea,
whatever passes along the paths of the seas.
O Lord, our Lord,
how majestic is your name in all the earth!
(Ps. 8:4-9).

Main Point

Human beings are the apex of God's creation
and have greater glory than the rest of creation.

Questions for Reflection

- How does the Bible's teaching that humans were created to reflect the glory of God give us purpose?
- What is the difference between what the Bible says about the uniqueness of humanity and what the rest of the world says about the uniqueness of humanity?

- How does (or, at least, how should) the Bible's teaching that humans are made in God's image affect the way we treat other people?

2. Glory Lost

In the last chapter we looked at humanity's unique glory of being created in God's image. While that is true, we must be humbled. Why? Well, if you've read the first three chapters of the Bible, you know why. If not, keep reading to discover another aspect of the creational glory of humanity. That glory has been tarnished with sin.

When Paul describes human sin, he puts it this way: 'all have sinned and fall short of the *glory* of God' (Rom. 3:23; emphasis mine). What does he mean by saying that we fall short of the glory of God? Part of what he means is what happened to our first parents in the Garden of Eden. Adam and Eve failed to obey the mandate given to them. They were not to eat of the Tree of the Knowledge of Good and Evil. Was it an apple tree, as many have suggested? We don't know. What matters is that they were told not to eat its fruit. It seems such a simple thing. There were trees of all kinds in Paradise, enough to satisfy them for eternity, but the grass is always greener on the other side. Their period of probation would have been changed into a permanent and sinless condition had they obeyed, but instead, they disobeyed and in doing so fell short of the glory of God. And God pronounced a curse on them and the land on which they trod.

It is important to note that we think of this story told in Genesis 3 as nothing less than actual history, including the part about a talking serpent! Bear in mind that he would have stood upright before the Fall, and any problem we may have with the idea of a talking creature is easily dispelled once we invoke God's supernatural ability to make it happen.

Moses describes the serpent as 'crafty' (Gen. 3:1). Did you spot that nowhere in Genesis does Moses call the serpent 'Satan?' That identification comes later (Rev. 12:9). What Adam and Eve saw was an animal of some kind, an animal that spoke! Far more important is *what* he said. There is an art to seduction. It involves pushing the envelope, just a little. Seduction creates a sense of entitlement, but with subtlety. The serpent twists God's word: 'Did God actually say, "You shall not eat of any tree in the garden"?' (Gen. 3:1). God had said nothing of the sort! He limited the command to one specific tree. Furthermore, He never said that they weren't allowed to touch it, and yet Eve adds this in her version of the command (Gen. 3:1). Presumably, they could have sat on the branches of the Tree; but they weren't allowed to eat its fruit.

Do you see what the serpent did? He made God's command stricter than it was. It was a form of legalism. And Eve snapped. And all of history changed as a consequence.

ADAM, EVE, AND HISTORY

Paul makes a great deal of Adam and his fall in Romans 5:12: 'Therefore, just as sin came into the world through one man, and death through sin, and so death spread to all men because all sinned.' Several issues need underlining from these words.

First, Paul most certainly regarded the story as history. What are the alternatives? That the entire chapter (and others in Genesis) are simply a fable, something like a mythic story after the fashion of J. R. R. Tolkien's *The Lord of the Rings*? Paul didn't think so. He puts

23

the Adam story alongside Jesus' death and resurrection. Both are historical facts.

Second, only an historical Fall in Eden can explain the origin of sin as far as humanity is concerned. Sin appears to have existed in the universe before Eden. After all, the serpent (aka the Devil) had already fallen from the angels. Without this account of the Fall we are left with only two alternatives: either sin is equally as pre-existent as good (a form of dualism), or God is the author of sin (which is unacceptable).

Third, when Paul says 'because all sinned' he is not saying that we sin in the same way that Adam did. That may be true in itself, but it is not what Paul is saying in Romans 5:12. The tense suggests something quite specific. We sinned *in Adam* in the sense that Adam was our representative head. And before you get hot and bothered at that suggestion— why should I suffer the consequences of another's failure?—we readily accept the other side of this argument: that Jesus is also our representative head. If the very idea of headship (or substitution) is offensive, then there is no good news for us.

Back to the story of Genesis 3. Eve saw how beautiful and aesthetically pleasing the fruit was. It probably had a very powerful and pleasing smell (Gen. 3:6). Adam, meanwhile, abdicated his responsibilities and allowed himself to be led by Eve and the serpent.

CURSES

The consequences of the disobedience were immediate. First came shame, and suddenly they are aware of each other's nakedness (Gen. 3:7). Next came a foreboding about God's presence, and they attempt to hide from Him—something humans are still doing (Gen. 3:8). Then came the blame game. Adam blames Eve (and by inference, God, who gave her to him). Eve blamed the serpent. The fellowship is broken, with each other and with God. Sin always seeks to break everything, including our relationships with those we love. Sibling rivalry and marital faithfulness are both strained by sin's disposition to put ourselves and our own needs ahead of others.

Then come the penalties. Eve will experience pain in childbirth and domestic strife (Gen. 3:16). Adam will experience hardship as he tills the land—the sense of frustration when the yield is far less than expected (Gen. 3:17-19). And then there's the ongoing war with the serpent (Gen. 3:14-15). They are all driven from Paradise with no possibility of return (Gen. 3:18-19). And to top it all, they will now grow old and experience death (Gen. 3:18-19).

The glory of Eden has departed. Adam and Eve are spiritually 'dead in their trespasses and sins' (Eph. 2:1). The next few chapters of history are filled with strife and violence until God answers with His great act of judgment, the Flood, which killed all but eight people (Gen. 4:1-9:17).

I know this all sounds bleak, but hang in there. Good news is ahead. But first, a bit more bad news.

ORIGINAL SIN

Sometimes the term 'original sin' is used to describe the events recorded above. More frequently, however, it is used to describe the corrupt nature that all of us inherit as a consequence of Adam's transgression. Every single human being is conceived in sin (cf. Ps. 51:5). This suggests more than simply a lack of righteousness; it is a built-in bias and propensity to break God's laws and seek our own way. Every human being, therefore, needs their sin to be forgiven.

In my own tradition, in which infants are baptized, I publicly ask the parents several questions, including the following: 'Do you acknowledge that your child is a sinner in need of the cleansing blood of Jesus Christ and of the Holy Spirit?' Just think about how counter-cultural that question is. Typically, these infants have yet to express a single word; but they are reckoned sinners, and in need of the gospel.

You may be thinking that this book started on such an encouraging note, only to throw you off a cliff. I understand. However, it's impossible for us to talk about glory, without talking about the sin of humanity. The good news of the gospel won't make sense without the bad news of our sin. Every human bears the stain of Adam's sin by nature and only the gospel of Jesus Christ can wash it away.

Main Point

Adam and Eve's sin shattered the image of God in us, but the remnants of this glory remain.

Questions for Reflection

- Why is it important that Genesis 3 reflects actual historical events?
- What are some ways that you have failed to reflect God's glory? Have you confessed these failures to God?

- What is fallen humanity's greatest need? *(Hint: This is one of those times when Jesus really is the answer!)*

3. Glory Restored

Christians often talk about being saved or being born again, but, have you ever thought, *what happens when a person is saved?* I mean, we know we go to heaven. We know we'll be with Jesus. But, have you given much thought to this reality?

Jesus once said, 'For the Son of Man came to seek and to save the lost' (Luke 19:10). So, what does it mean to be saved? We will need to address this question in more detail again in a subsequent chapter, but for now, I want us to think along the lines of where we left off in the previous chapter. There, we saw that when Adam and Eve fell, there were massive consequences. They were not what they were before the Fall. Things changed.

SHATTERED IMAGES

So, here's a question: did Adam and Eve lose their status as image-bearers after the Fall? The answer is not a simple yes or no. It's one of those questions that requires some nuancing. It depends on what you mean by image-bearers. Here, it is important to understand image-bearing in two categories. The first is the *narrow* sense and the second is the *broad* sense.

Take, for example, what Paul says in Colossians and Ephesians:

Do not lie to one another, seeing that you have put off the old self with its practices and have put on the new self, which is being renewed in knowledge after the image of its creator (Col. 3:9-10).

Be renewed in the spirit of your minds, and… put on the new self, created after the likeness of God in true righteousness and holiness (Eph. 4:23-24).

Paul is talking about what happens at conversion and uses the language of image-bearing. The image of God was *lost* as a consequence of sin and is restored as a consequence of conversion. We are renewed in *knowledge*, *true righteousness*, and *holiness*. The 'new self' has these qualities that the 'old self' did not. Christians know God and demonstrate genuine aspects of godly behavior. That is, they 'bear fruit' in their daily lives.

Putting this another way, when we are saved—when we believe that Jesus is God's Son and that He died on the cross for our sins—the fallen state of our image-bearing is restored. This is to view the image of God in a *narrow* sense.[1]

There is also image-bearing in a broad sense. To consider this second category, think back to a previous chapter. If you remember, we saw that the image-bearing status of Adam and Eve was also seen in their exercise of

---

1   I am a minister in a Presbyterian church. In my church, and many other Presbyterian churches, we use a document called the Westminster Confession of Faith to summarize what we believe. I think the Confession's definition of the image of God in the narrow sense is helpful: 'After God had made all other creatures, he created man, male and female, with reasonable and immortal souls, endued with knowledge, righteousness, and true holiness after his own image, having the law of God written in their hearts, and power to fulfill it; and yet under a possibility of transgressing, being left to the liberty of their own will, which was subject unto change. Besides this law written in their hearts, they received a command not to eat of the tree of the knowledge of good and evil; which while they kept were happy in their communion with God, and had dominion over the creatures.' (Westminster Confession of Faith, 4:2).

dominion over the earth. While this dominion was severely hampered as a consequence of Adam's sin and God's subsequent curse, it was not wholly eradicated.

For example, just look around at humans today. Unregenerate women and men continue to explore the universe, discover new medicines, harness previously unknown sources of energy, compose beautiful music, write books, and perform amazing athletic skills, all of which demonstrate image-bearing. We may think of this aspect of the image of God as the *broader* sense. And in this sense, the image of God is not lost as a consequence of the Fall.

PROGRESS

Why all this talk about the narrow and broad sense of what it means to be image-bearers? Well, the renewed status of humanity's image-bearing *in the narrow sense* is not fully complete at the time of conversion. There is an aspect of progress and advancement to be considered. Listen to what Paul says:

And we all, with unveiled face, beholding the glory of the Lord, are being transformed into the same image from one degree of glory to another. For this comes from the Lord who is the Spirit (2 Cor. 3:18).

Among many other matters addressed in this verse, not least the divine nature of the Holy Spirit, Paul is advocating that the renewed image-bearing status of the 'new self' (Eph. 4:24) is ongoing and progressive and does not come to fulness until we are glorified. How is this achieved, exactly? The answer seems to be that Christians, those who live in the New Testament era, have a clearer understanding of spiritual realities, especially the glory of God. By beholding this glory in Jesus, the ministry of the Holy Spirit and now the completed Scripture, we are being transformed more and more into the likeness of Jesus, who is the true image of God (2 Cor. 4:4; Col. 1:15). (We will return to this idea in another chapter.)

From one point of view, our on-going transformation (or 'sanctification') is a matter of becoming more like Jesus.[2] Think once again of what Paul writes in Romans 8:29:

---

2   For more on the topic of 'sanctification' be sure to check out RYM's other book in the Track series, *A Student's Guide to Sanctification.*

For those whom he foreknew he also predestined to be conformed to the image of his Son, in order that he might be the firstborn among many brothers.

We are being conformed to the image of Jesus. The goal of sanctification is Jesus-likeness. There is a sense in which we may think of sanctification as a judge's verdict: final and complete. Paul tells the Corinthians (the most dysfunctional church in the New Testament!) that they are 'sanctified in Christ Jesus' (1 Cor. 1:2). Clearly, he is saying that something definitive has occurred in their lives. They have been set apart and forgiven in Christ. They are a 'new creation' (2 Cor. 5:17). We sometimes call this aspect of sanctification *definitive* or *positional* sanctification.

But in 2 Corinthians 3:18, another aspect of sanctification is in view, an aspect that grows and alters. In the progressive nature of our relationship with Jesus, we are being changed 'from one degree of glory to another.'

At least, that is how it should appear. There is a sense in which our holiness should *advance*. It ought to be true of us that we are holier today than we were a year ago. Sadly, this is not always the case. In the struggle that is sanctification we sense, too often, the tension of the apostle, 'For I do not do what I want, but I do the very thing I hate' (Rom. 7:15). Progressive sanctification is not necessarily an upward straight-line graph; rather, it rolls, twists, and turns as we wrestle against the world, the flesh, and the devil (cf. Eph. 2:2-3).

Christians really are glorious creatures! And there's more glory to come.

Main Point

God's plan to save His people will restore the glory they had before the Fall.

Questions for Reflection

- In what sense can we say that the image of God in humankind was broken at the Fall? In what sense should we affirm that humans bear God's image even after the Fall?
- How is the biblical idea of 'sanctification' different from (and better than) the contemporary notion of 'self-actualization' or 'self-fulfillment'?
- In what ways are you striving to be more Jesus-like?

4. The Golden Chain

What would you say are some of the most encouraging words of Scripture? This can be a dangerous question to ask, because all of Scripture is written by God. To be sure, there may be certain sections of Scripture that offer you unique blessing because of your season of life or upbringing. Regardless of where you are in life, reflect on the encouragement of these following verses:

For those whom he foreknew he also predestined to be conformed to the image of his Son, in order that he might be the firstborn among many brothers. And those whom he predestined he also called, and those whom he called he also justified, and those whom he justified he also glorified (Rom. 8:29-30).

These are some of the most comforting words in the Bible. They guarantee that what God begins, He completes. They form the basis of our assurance of salvation. God doesn't give up on His children. Without the promise of Romans 8, we would be left to work things out on our own, and we would be swallowed up by uncertainty.

In the late sixteenth century, a puritan scholar-preacher who taught at Cambridge University in England wrote a book based on these words, called *The Golden Chain*. The five elements in these verses—foreknowledge, predestination, calling, justification and glorification—are linked together, forming a chain of events that culminates in the eventual glorification of God's children.

There is an order to salvation. And there are more elements in the 'chain' than are mentioned here—for example, faith, repentance, adoption, sanctification (in more than one sense), and perseverance. Theologians refer to this chain using the Latin expression, ordo salutis (the order of salvation).

Some things precede other things logically and, to some extent, temporally. For example, before we can exercise faith, we need to be *regenerated*. We are 'dead in our trespasses' by nature (Eph. 2:5). We lack the ability to respond to God's gracious offer of mercy. Paul makes it clear: 'For by grace you have been saved through faith. And this is not your own doing; it is the gift of God, not a result of works, so that no one may boast' (Eph. 2:8-9). So, God must first soften our hard hearts to make us able to respond to Him in faith. This softening is called 'regeneration'. We already see something of an order emerging: regeneration—faith.

LINKS OF A CHAIN

These verses from Romans 8 introduce five distinguishable aspects of our salvation and suggest a logical order. In doing so, they go outside of our current experience and back into eternity. Think about that: God's plan to save you comes from eternity past! That should blow your mind! It also raises two separate but related aspects of our salvation: Foreknowledge and predestination. Before we talk about the 'p' word, let's talk about *foreknowledge*.

Foreknowledge simply means knowledge that someone has before an event. In this instance God 'knew' us before we were born. That's not difficult to understand since God exists in eternity and knows everything. 'Great is our Lord, and abundant in power; his understanding is beyond measure' (Ps. 147:5).

But there is something more subtle about the use of the word 'foreknowledge' here. God foreknows individuals. It is very specific. And the knowledge in view here is more than mere intellectual knowledge. In the Old Testament, knowledge is associated with relationship and love. Think of the way Genesis describes the birth of Cain: 'Now Adam knew Eve his wife, and she conceived and bore Cain' (Gen. 4:1). To 'know' in this sense is very intimate indeed! God's foreknowledge is a sign of His affection for us, *beforehand*. He set His love upon us in eternity. Our salvation, then, is not some later decision, some 'Johnny come lately' affair.

Having set His love upon us, He sets the course of our destiny. He predestines us. Now before we introduce all kinds of objections to this idea, several things need to be said:

First, what *guarantee* of future glory can we have if, when all is said and done, we are the masters of our own destiny? How good are you at keeping your promise? If we're honest, our record at keeping promises isn't a good one, and there are a thousand obstacles to get over before the future glory of heaven. No, the only *guarantee* of glory is that God promises and secures it. Think of the verse before the passages we are considering: 'And we know that for those who love God all things work together for good, for those who are called according to his purpose' (Rom. 8:28). That verse is meant to be an encouragement for us when we find ourselves at the mercy of some trial or other. God has got this! His plan hasn't suddenly become unraveled. It doesn't matter whether we understand what He's doing; it only matters that He understands what He's doing!

Second, The New Testament talks a lot about predestination and election. Consider the following:

He chose us in him [Christ] before the foundation of the world (Eph. 1:4).

He predestined us for adoption (Eph. 1:5).

We have obtained an inheritance, having been predestined according to the purpose of him who works all things according to the counsel of his will (Eph. 1:11).

Even Jesus Himself talked about predestination:

For many are called, but few are chosen (Matt. 22:14).

All things have been handed over to me by my Father, and no one knows the Son except the Father, and no one knows the Father except the Son and anyone to whom the Son chooses to reveal him (Matt. 11:27).

One way or another, the Bible insists that God has a plan that He executes flawlessly.

THE 'P' WORD

Now, many get hot and bothered over the doctrine of predestination because it seems to suggest the loss of human freedom. It reduces us to robots. But again, this is *not* what Scripture teaches. On the contrary, we have the power to choose. Whether we wear shoes or flip-flops may be a trivial example, but it *is* an example of a real choice. We make thousands of them every day. And, moreover, we are held morally accountable for the choices we make. It is the basis of justice: good ought to be rewarded; evil ought to be punished.

But how? How can we choose if God chooses? How is human freedom and divine sovereignty compatible? The Bible doesn't answer this question. Indeed, it sometimes places the two truths right up against each other without so much as blinking the eye: 'work out your own salvation with fear and trembling, for it is God who works in you, both to will and to work for his good pleasure' (Phil. 2:12b-13). Human effort and divine sovereignty must be compatible, even if we don't know exactly how that can be. (Remember, God is infinite and we are finite. He should blow our minds from time to time.)

Did you notice how Paul moves into our world of space and time after he mentions predestination in Romans 8:29-30? He mentions our calling and our justification. In an interesting section at the very beginning of Paul's letter to the Corinthians, Paul mentions how the Corinthian Christians were called into a relationship with the Lord Jesus Christ. 'To the church of God that is in Corinth, to those sanctified in Christ Jesus, called to be saints' (1 Cor. 1:2). The expression 'called to be saints' can equally be translated 'the holy called ones.' Instead of being labelled 'a Christian,' I could equally be labelled 'a called one'! I am one whom the Holy Spirit has called into union and fellowship with Jesus. And having been called into this relationship, I am justified. I stand in a right relationship with God. 'Therefore, since we have been justified by faith, we have peace with God through our Lord Jesus Christ' (Rom. 5:1).

And from justification Paul draws a straight line to future glory, but he puts it in a tense that suggests it is already ours: 'and those whom he justified he also glorified.' The golden chain.

Some of you may be asking, but isn't our glorification something for the future? Yes and no. Yes, our ultimate glorification is in the future, but there is a sense in which the future is so certain (predestination *again*), that we can be assured of it *right now*. This is why I began by saying this is one of the most encouraging sections of Scripture! Christians are 'raised up' with Christ and are sitting 'with him in the heavenly places' (Eph. 2:6). The glory which shall be revealed in us is viewed as a *'done deal'* finished, complete, and secure—praise God!

Main Point

What God begins, He promises to complete.

Questions for Reflection

- In what ways does the fact the God foreknew you drive home the graciousness of salvation?

- Read all of Romans chapter 8. How does Paul use the doctrine of predestination as a source of encouragement in Romans 8?
- What is the basis of our assurance of future glorification?

5. Now and Not Yet

God's world is a beautiful one for sure. But, it is broken and evidence of that is all around. Abortion is an evil that murders infants each day. Cancer continues to claim lives as doctors search for a cure. Racism is a reality that impacts every culture across the globe. Divorce continues to sow seeds of pain in future generations. This world is beautiful, but sad.

This world, however, is not our home, but it will be. We are pilgrims marching through this world to a better land—the new heaven and new earth that Isaiah depicts in the closing two chapters of his magnificent prophecy. We are homesick for our true abode. We long to be free from pain and disease, strife and opposition, sin and Satan. We find ourselves in a strange condition. A condition theologians refer to as the *now* and *not yet*.

In one sense, something of the age to come has already occurred. Already, in Christ, we are a 'new creation' (2 Cor. 5:17), bearing God's glory. Something of our eventual home has already manifested itself.

Think of how John puts it: 'Beloved, we are God's children now, and what we will be has not yet appeared; but we know that when he appears we shall be like him, because we shall see him as he is' (1 John 3:2). We are God's children now. What will be true *then* is true already! There is glory to come, but we are already a people of glory (2 Cor. 3:18). This was spoken of in the previous chapter.

Think of the way Jesus talks about the kingdom of God. 'But if it is by the finger of God that I cast out demons, then the kingdom of God has come upon you' (Luke 11:20). Clearly in this instance, Jesus is saying that the kingdom was already present in His miraculous ministry. But think of how He taught us to pray in the Lord's Prayer: 'Your kingdom come' (Matt. 6:10). In this instance, the kingdom has not yet fully arrived! So, which is it? Has the kingdom arrived or is it yet future? The answer is *both*. The kingdom was *inaugurated* at Jesus' coming, but it won't find its final form until the end of the ages.

Or think of the way Paul says that Christians have 'every spiritual blessing in Christ' (Eph. 1:3) and yet need to keep being filled with the Spirit (Eph. 5:18). Or the way Paul speaks of Christians having died to sin (Rom. 6:2) and at the same time find that 'sin...dwells within me' (Rom. 7:20). All of these examples reveal how we live in the tension between the *now* and the *not yet*. Rest assured, the Bible is not contradicting itself.

SOVEREIGNTY AND RESPONSIBILITY

That said, sometimes the tension can seem to be at the edge of contradiction. We are

- already adopted in Christ (Rom. 8:15), but not yet adopted (Rom. 8:23)
- already redeemed in Christ (Eph. 1:7), but not yet redeemed (Eph. 4:30)
- already sanctified in Christ (1 Cor. 1:2), but not yet sanctified (1 Thess. 5:23–24)
- already saved in Christ (Eph. 2:8), but not yet saved (Rom. 5:9)
- already raised with Christ (Eph. 2:6), but not yet raised (1 Cor. 15:52)

This has proved to be something of a challenge. Even in New Testament days, there were those who thought that everything was all *now*. In Corinth, for example, the distribution of gifts made them think that heaven had already come. It led to pride issues. Theologians call it *over-realized eschatology*. It partly explains their raucous behavior. They thought they could do whatever they liked with their bodies, otherwise God wouldn't have blessed them in the way that He had. And so, for 29 chapters, Paul spells it out. The kingdom is now and not yet. They might speak in tongues, but they were 'children,' and not in a good way (1 Cor. 14:20). This over-confident stance can lead to prideful expectations of the 'Victorious Christian life.' We may mistakenly believe that we have conquered sin and are no longer subject to its tempting and alluring powers.

Alternatively, this 'over-realized eschatology' can have a very different effect. If the *now* is filled with trials and difficulties, we can easily become discouraged. We can lose sight of the blessings and certainty of the glory that lies ahead.

John Newton in the eighteenth century summarized what we are thinking about in this way:

I am not what I ought to be—ah, how imperfect and deficient! I am not what I wish to be—I abhor what is evil, and I would cleave to what is good! I am not what I hope to be—soon, soon shall I put off mortality, and with mortality all sin and imperfection. Yet, though I am not what I ought to be, nor what I wish to be, nor what I hope to be, I can truly say, I am not what I once was; a slave to sin and Satan; and I can heartily join with the apostle, and acknowledge, 'By the grace of God I am what I am.' [1]

One prominent theologian in the twentieth century used the analogy of D-Day and V-Day to illustrate the tension between the *now* and the *not yet*. The invasion of Normandy on June 6, 1944 was one of the bravest battles in military history. The success of the Allied troops, at considerable cost, spelled the end of Nazi control over Europe. To all intents and purposes, the war was won. But it would be

---

1   Josiah Bull, *The Life of John Newton* (Edinburgh: Banner of Truth, 2007), p. 289.

another year before final victory was attained in Europe and even longer for the war in the Far East to cease. When Jesus died and rose again, destroying the works of the devil (1 John 3:8), He inaugurated D-Day. Effectively, the battle was won. But the devil continues to prowl about seeking whom he may devour (1 Pet. 5:8). V-Day has not arrived, but the future is certain.

FIRSTFRUITS

We can summarize it this way. Those who are regenerated and find themselves 'in Christ' have a foretaste of the blessings of the age to come, and a pledge and guarantee of the resurrection body. However, what we have right now are the 'firstfruits' (Rom. 8:23; 1 Cor. 15:20; James 1:18). We are the first agricultural crop that promises a larger harvest to come.

The glory has begun in us, but the fullness of glory is not yet.

Main Point

Christians continue to struggle against sin in this world, but through Christ's victory we can also bear fruit for Him 'now' as we wait for the 'not yet.'

Questions for Reflection

- How are you encouraged by the Bible's teaching that while we still struggle with sin, it won't have the last word for those who trust in Jesus?

- Have you ever noticed the tension in the Bible between divine sovereignty and human responsibility? Why is it important to balance these two facts in a biblical way?

- What are some ways that you experience the firstfruits of glorification right now?

6. The Glory in Us

There is something which Peter writes in his second epistle that has caused the church a great deal of confusion. Indeed, it divided the Western and Eastern churches in the early centuries of the Christian church and continues to do so. This is what Peter wrote:

> *His divine power has granted to us all things that pertain to life and godliness, through the knowledge of him who called us to his own glory and excellence, by which he has granted to us his precious and very great promises, so that through them you may become partakers of the divine nature, having escaped from the corruption that is in the world because of sinful desire (2 Pet. 1:3-4).*

What does Peter mean when he says that we have been 'called to his own glory' and 'become partakers of the divine nature'? What kind of glory is this?

Our destiny as Christians is to share the glory of God. In the tension between the *now* and the *not yet*, we continually fall short of this glory (Rom. 3:23). We participate in this glory now, but not yet in its final and fully glorious form. 'Beloved, we are God's children now, and what we will be has not yet appeared; but we know that when he appears we shall be like him, because we shall see him as he is. And everyone who thus hopes in him purifies himself as he is pure' (1 John 3:2-3).

If you are a Christian, you are indwelt by the Holy Spirit. He makes His home in us. Jesus emphasized it in the Upper Room: 'And I will ask the Father, and he will give you another Helper, to be with you forever, even the Spirit of truth, whom the world cannot receive, because it neither sees him nor knows him. You know him, for he dwells with you and will be in you' (John 14:16-17).

And Jesus meant us to understand that by sending the Holy Spirit He ensures His own presence in us. The Spirit is Jesus' representative agent. The very same Spirit that lived in the man Jesus now lives in us. His indwelling ensures that we are in Christ and that Christ is in us. Jesus put it this way: 'The glory that you have given me I have given to them, that they may be one even as we are one, I in them and you in me, that they may become perfectly one, so that the world may know that you sent me and loved them even as you loved me' (John 17:22-23).

Try and wrap your mind around this—Jesus in us, the Spirit in us, the Trinity in us! We have an intimate relation of glory in the Father, Son, and Holy Spirit. And it is a relationship that will culminate in future glory where we will share in His glory. Created in the image of God, we are to be fully restored to reflect that image in the glory to come.

DIVINIZATION?

Let's be clear as to what Peter is *not* saying. He is not saying that somehow or another our human nature is divinized. We are not divine. Christians are not gods in any sense. The word translated 'partakers' in 2 Peter 1:4 is the Greek word that is translated elsewhere as *fellowship*. Since the divine nature of the Holy Spirit indwells us, we can say that we fellowship with the divine nature. We have the most intimate relationship and bond with the divine nature of God.

In the Eastern Church, sometimes known as the Orthodox Church, the theological term for what we are thinking about here is *theōsis*. And in some of the early Church Fathers, *theōsis* sometimes led to language that some regarded as a form of deification. That is, that Christians are little deities (gods). In recent days, some in the Western church have begun to use the term carefully by insisting that *theōsis* does not involve either deification (we become divine) or some mixture of the human and divine, 'like ingredients in an ontological soup.'[1]

UNION WITH CHRIST

Another way of expressing the way we fellowship with the glory of God is through the phrase 'union with Christ'. Paul talks about union with Christ a lot. Preachers often point out that he employs the phrase 'in Christ' 164 times in his letters. For example, in Romans 8:1 he says, 'there is therefore now no condemnation for those who are *in Christ Jesus'* (emphasis mine).

---

1   Robert Letham, *Systematic Theology* (Wheaton, IL: Crossway, 2019), 776.

It is not difficult to see why this phrase is so much a part of his DNA. After Saul of Tarsus encountered Stephen, an encounter that led to Stephen's death, Saul heard a voice saying to him, 'Saul, Saul, why are you persecuting me?' (Acts 9:4). And when Saul asked as to the identity of the voice, he was told, 'I am Jesus, whom you are persecuting' (Acts 9:5). Could you imagine the guilt Paul felt over killing Stephen? I doubt that Paul ever laid his head down at night to sleep without thinking of his involvement in that terrible death. He had laid hands on Stephen, but in effect, he had laid his hands upon Jesus. Stephen was 'in Christ' and Christ was in Stephen! He had laid his hands on the glory of God.

Our destiny is that we are to be like God, not in the sense that our humanity is to become divine, but in terms of our holiness. One day, we shall be free from sin and all its effects. We will be as holy as God is holy. In a sense, in terms of our justification, that is already true. In Christ, we are reckoned 'the righteousness of God' (2 Cor. 5:21). Using a different analogy, we are clothed with Christ's spotless garment of righteousness. We have 'put on Christ' (Gal. 3:27). But we are not entirely holy; nor shall we be until we get to the other side of this present evil world.

Now we fellowship with the Father, Son, and Holy Spirit, but that fellowship is veiled: 'For now we see in a mirror dimly, but then face to face. Now I know in part; then I shall know fully, even as I have been fully known' (1 Cor. 13:12).

It is a glorious thing to be a Christian! We need to remind ourselves frequently of our current status and look forward with eager expectation to what is promised to us in the gospel.

Main Point

Christians are united to Christ and indwelt by the Holy Spirit.

Questions for Reflection

- You have three seconds to answer the following question: 'what does it mean to be a Christian?'
- After reading this chapter, how is union with Christ central to Christianity?
- How does the fact that Christians are united to Christ and indwelt by the Holy Spirit change the way you live the Christian life?

- How does the fact that all Christians are united to Christ change the way you think about, speak about, and treat other people?

7. The Glory and Glorification of Jesus

As we've already said, Scripture does not contradict itself. While that's true, we can still say that there are difficult truths in the Bible. One of those truths is the incarnation. All sorts of confusion, debate, and heresy has occurred from people trying to understand God taking on flesh.

God's own glory shines in the face of Jesus. 'For God, who said, "Let light shine out of darkness," has shone in our hearts to give the light of the knowledge of the glory of God in the face of Jesus Christ' (2 Cor. 4:6). We know that now, but it wasn't immediately evident when He walked this earth. His glory was veiled, to Himself and to others. After all, He didn't look like God to those who encountered Him, at least, not initially. Paul, in speaking of the incarnation, put it this way:

who, though he was in the form of God,
did not count equality with God a thing to
be grasped,
but emptied himself,
by taking the form of a servant,
being born in the likeness of men.
And being found in human form,
he humbled himself by becoming obedient to
the point of death,
even death on a cross (Phil. 2:6-8).

He emptied Himself. That's a literal translation of what Paul wrote. Some translations shy away from the implication that He emptied Himself of some aspect of His divine nature and employ a euphemism instead: 'he made himself of no reputation.' This translation is conveying the correct thought, but it is not what Paul wrote.

He emptied Himself, not by subtraction, but by addition. In addition to being divine, He was also human. And such was the reality of His humanity, that He did not always appear to be divine. When Jesus ate fish or went to sleep, these were the actions of a man, not God. The disciples had to *believe* that He is divine. We could say that His divine nature was veiled. If you've ever seen anyone with a veil, you understand the comparison.

THE TRANSFIGURATION

In order to help us understand how it is that now we see the glory of God shining in Jesus' face, we need to take a look at the Transfiguration. Let's take Luke's account of it.

Now about eight days after these sayings he took with him Peter and John and James and went up on the mountain to pray. And as he was praying, the appearance of his face was altered, and his clothing became dazzling white. And behold, two men were talking with him, Moses and Elijah, who appeared in glory and spoke of his departure, which he was about to accomplish at Jerusalem. Now Peter and those who were with him were heavy with sleep, but when they became fully awake they saw his glory and the two men who stood with him. And as the men were parting from him, Peter said to Jesus, 'Master, it is good that we are here. Let us make three tents, one for you and one for Moses and one for Elijah'—not knowing what he said. As he was saying these things, a cloud came and overshadowed them, and they were afraid as they entered the cloud. And a voice came out of the cloud, saying, 'This is my Son, my Chosen One; listen to him!' And when the voice had spoken, Jesus was found alone. And they kept silent and told no one in those days anything of what they had seen (Luke 9:28-36).

We must be selective in what we deduce from this passage, so let's simply focus on what happened to Jesus' body in this incident. Luke says that His face was 'altered' and that 'his clothing became dazzling white.' He also tells us that some kind of fissure—a rent in space—appeared and Moses and Elijah walked through and 'appeared in glory.' Later, having fallen asleep (how could they possibly have done that?!), they awoke, 'they saw his glory.'

What happened?

Something happened to Jesus' body! He was 'transfigured.' Literally, His body experienced a *metamorphosis.* Luke does not explain it. He simply records it. Therefore, we must be careful of reading too much into this.

At one level, we are used to seeing people's countenance change. They may appear happy or sad. We may infer that they are 'under the weather' today. Luke is stating something far more than that! Perhaps a clue might be the way Moses' face shone when he encountered the glory cloud on Mount Sinai (and remember he's here in this story, too). Something of the glory of God was shining in Moses' face, too.

Do you recall what Luke said when Jesus was born in Bethlehem? Following the angelic announcement of Jesus' birth, Luke added, 'the glory of the Lord shone around them' (Luke 2:9). And when Peter reflected on the Transfiguration, years later, he said, 'we were eye-witnesses of his majesty' (2 Pet. 1:16).

We need to be clear that Jesus' humanity will always remain such. At no point does His human nature become something else. The Transfiguration isn't Jesus 'becoming God'. The change must be compatible with His retention of a full and complete human nature.

But, as we will see in the next chapter, our own bodies are going to be different in the glory that is to come. It is perfectly possible, therefore, that for a moment at least, Jesus was given a glimpse of the body He now has in glory, a body free from the stresses and strains of life in a fallen world.

Since Moses and Elijah came to speak to Him about His death (the English word 'departure' translates the Greek word for *exodus*), it might seem altogether appropriate that Jesus might need a brief glimpse of what He could expect on the other side of death. In the limitations of His human nature, it is perfectly reasonable to think that Jesus might need some encouragement. This truth should be a deep encouragement to believers. Our Savior took our weaknesses on Himself and knows what it means to need encouragement.

At the Transfiguration, and at His resurrection appearances, we catch a glimpse of the glorified Jesus. He remains human and divine. The two natures are never confused, or to employ the negatives of the Chalcedonian Creed of AD 451, the two natures exist 'without confusion, without change, without division, without separation.' Jesus' human nature will stay fully human for the rest of eternity. The human nature did not become less human at the Transfiguration. Instead, Jesus was given a preview of what glorified humanity will be like. As Christians, we have the sure hope that 'when He appears, we will be like Him [glorified], because we shall see Him as He is' (1 John 3:2). Isn't Jesus a glorious savior?

Main Point

Although He looked like any other man, Scripture shows us that Jesus is the glory of God.

Questions for Reflection

- Reflect on what Philippians 2:1-11 says about Jesus. What does this tell you about the character of God?
- How does the Transfiguration dispel the notion that Jesus was merely a great teacher?
- Why is it important that Jesus is both fully human and fully divine?

8. Future Glory

What does your body look like?

That question makes most of us uncomfortable. While I don't want to create any dissatisfaction with your body, I think most of us have some aspects we would like to change. We need to know that God created our bodies, so we must be cautious of critiquing His creation. At the same time, maybe our dissatisfaction with our current bodies has a link to our body's future glory?

Earlier, we took a glimpse at the *order* in which our salvation is applied. We noted that in Romans 8:29, *glorification* is the final link in the chain that describes how redemption is applied to us. We noted, too, that our eventual glorification is so certain that Paul states it in a way that suggests it has already happened. There are *now* and *not yet* aspects to glorification.

What can we expect in our own glorification? Before we proceed any further, we need to be clear what we are asking. And here we run into differing viewpoints about end-time matters. I can only relate my own understanding here.

Unless Jesus comes before we die, our glorification will be in two distinct stages. The first stage involves asking what happens to a believer 5 seconds after they die (I chose 5 seconds at random). The answer is clear. We will be in heaven. Our bodies will still be here on earth, but *we* (our conscious self) will be with Jesus. You may say it this way: our *souls* will be in heaven. Again, this is what will happen if we die *before* Jesus returns.

Let's get some biblical support for that. Think of Jesus' words to the dying thief: 'Truly, I say to you, today you will be with me in paradise' (Luke 23:43). Or, think of Paul's words to the Corinthians: 'away from the body and at home with the Lord' (2 Cor. 5:6, 8).

Heaven is not our final home. That will be the new heavens and new earth which we will think about in the next chapter. Heaven is an intermediate existence. It is where the human body of Jesus is right now. Remember, His human body can only be in one zip-code. His human nature is not ubiquitous (it cannot be everywhere). That is a property that belongs to His divine nature alone.

HEAVEN

What is heaven like? And more pertinently for our theme in these pages, what will glorification in this intermediate state look like? In one sense, it will be incomplete.

We will be absent from the body. We will exist only in our soulishness. The church, for the most part, has affirmed this point of view. Some, however, have put great stress on the tense of the verb in 2 Corinthians 5:1: 'For we know that if the tent that is our earthly home is destroyed, *we have* a building from God, a house not made with hands, eternal in the heavens.' The tense of the verb 'we have' may imply some kind of temporary physical body that falls short of the resurrection body. After all, it is difficult to conceive how we will move, see, or hear without legs, eyes, or ears.

First and foremost, we shall see Jesus, for this is His current home. And we will be reunited with all those believers (Old and New Testament believers) who have already died. Furthermore, many (possibly most!) Christians also believe that children who die in infancy as well as those incapacitated through cognitive inabilities will be in heaven. And, of course, we will see creatures that we have never seen (at least, not knowingly): angels and archangels, cherubim and seraphim.

Where is heaven? That's a great question, and the easiest answer is to say, it is *somewhere*. It is where the human body of Jesus is. It is a part of the created universe. We typically talk about heaven as 'up there,' probably because Jesus ascended into the cloud. But I like to think of it as a universe that is parallel to this one. It is from this location that Moses and Elijah appeared through 'a rent in space' to speak to Jesus on the Mount of Transfiguration.

If we take, for a moment, the parable of the rich man and Lazarus, a parable that describes the *intermediate state* or *heaven*, one thing is sure: they were both conscious of their surroundings and furthermore, they seem to be conscious of events on earth (Luke 16:19-31).

Most importantly, there is no sin in heaven. To cite the *Shorter Catechism*,

> Q. What benefits do believers receive from Christ at death?

A. The souls of believers are at their death made perfect in holiness, and do immediately pass into glory; and their bodies, being still united to Christ, do rest in their graves till the resurrection.[1]

SLEEPING

What, then, are we to make of those occasions when the Bible describes death as 'sleep'? These are just a few examples:

- Describing a localized resurrection of the dead that occurred in Jerusalem after Jesus' resurrection, Matthew says, 'many bodies of the saints who had *fallen asleep* were raised' (Matt. 27:52).
- Jesus said of Jairus' deceased twelve-year old daughter, 'she is not dead but *sleeping*' (Luke 8:52).
- Jesus said (when talking to His disciples about Lazarus, who had been dead for two days), 'Our friend Lazarus has *fallen asleep*, but I go to awaken him' (John 11:11).
- When Stephen was stoned to death, Luke writes, 'he fell asleep' (Acts 7:60).
- Recalling the witnesses to the Resurrection of Christ, Paul mentions 'five hundred

---

1   Q & A 37.

brothers' who saw him 'at once,' adding 'some have *fallen asleep*' (1 Cor. 15:6).

- Paul urges the Thessalonians, 'we do not want you to be uninformed, brothers, about those who are *asleep*, that you may not grieve as others do who have no hope' (1 Thess. 4:13).

Except in the case of violent death, most people close their eyes when they die and appear to go to sleep. This is just a figure of speech, and it does not necessitate that we understand this as being some form of soul-sleep, where believers are unconscious in the intermediate state.

Heaven is a condition of glory, but it is not our final experience of it. That experience will be the new heavens and new earth. And that truth is what we will discuss in the next chapter.

Main Point

Heaven is a glorious place, but it is only a waiting room before the new heavens and new earth.

Questions for Reflection

- Reflect on Jesus' parable about the Lazarus and the rich man in Luke 16:19-31. How does the reality of life after death impact the way you live now?

- Reflect on 1 Thessalonians 4:13-18. How does the Bible's teaching about heaven help us to grieve as those who have hope?
- How does the gospel inform a Christian view of death? How is this different from what the rest of the world thinks about death?

9. Final Glory

━━━

Have you ever been to France? China? Australia? Antarctica? There are places on this earth that we'd like to visit, but probably won't get the chance to. Maybe time or money will keep us from visiting these places. Whatever your 'dream destination' may be, there's a longing attached to that.

Well, the Bible tells us that there is a destination awaiting those who believe in Jesus as their Lord and Savior. And, ultimately, that's the destination that fulfills any longing we have on this earth.

Every believer will experience final glorification *at the same time*. At the Second Coming of Jesus, the trumpet will sound, and our bodies will rise. We will be given resurrection bodies, bodies fit for the new existence of what the Bible calls 'the new heaven and new earth' (Isa. 65:17; 66:22; 2 Pet. 3:13; Rev. 21:1).

When people ask, 'What is heaven like?', they typically confuse the intermediate state (what we really mean by heaven) and the final state (the new heaven and new earth).

Yes, a new *earth*! This present one all cleaned up and made better. Press the image and make it solid—an earth with rocks and hills, oceans and rivers, forests and fields, birds and animals. And the resurrected bodies of the saints now reunited with their conscious souls.

In Romans 8:19-22, Paul makes a great deal of how the earth, cursed by the Fall, longs to be re-born and made new. Adam was created to subdue the universe, explore its possibilities, and harness its powers for good. In the new earth, the glorified saints will continue this work. For eternity, redeemed humanity will discover more and more of God's universe and as *viceregent*, rule the universe and glorify God in the process.

The final two chapters of Revelation depict the future existence in terms of a city-temple in which 'the glory of God' shines (Rev. 21:11; cf. 21:22-23; 22:5). And since the Greek word (and for that matter, the same is true of the

Hebrew word) for 'glory' suggests *weightiness*, the streets of the city will be full of weightiness and God's presence with His people.

PURITY AS NEVER BEFORE

In this brave new world, there will be absolute purity and perfection: 'No longer will there be anything accursed' (Rev. 22:3). Because Jesus was made a curse for us, there is nothing left of the curse in the redeemed universe (cf. Gal. 3:13).

Can you imagine a world without the least trace of sin? Frankly, though I try to, it is difficult. What a thrilling existence that will be!

And what will our resurrected bodies be like? New and improved is my answer. What aspects of current humanity are utterly incapacitated by sin and its crippling effects? I should imagine they are many. But in thinking about enhancements to our current experience of humanness, we should not forget that there will be many aspects of continuity.

Take the resurrection of Jesus, for example, and Paul's hint that His resurrection is a 'firstfruits' of our own resurrection (1 Cor. 15:20). We can confidently expect that His resurrection body may well be the model for our own.

At one level, nothing is different. He was subject to the laws of gravity as He walked the Emmaus Road with those two downcast disciples. Moreover, when He got to Emmaus, He broke bread with them. After all, what was the first thing He asked the disciples in the Upper Room following His resurrection appearance to Mary? 'Do you have anything to eat?' (Luke 24:41). Astonishing? Not really. He had been dead for three days and now His stomach was empty. Later He would eat fish in Galilee with the disciples (Luke 24:40-43; John 21:1-19). Note that He was not a vegetarian, even in the state of His resurrected body!

At other points, there is discontinuity. Does the fact that He possessed the ability to pass through closed doors (if, indeed, the text demands this interpretation) suggest that the laws of physics in the new heaven and earth may well have some aspects that we currently do not experience (Luke 24:36; John 20:19, 26)? Perhaps.

A BODY OF GLORY

Paul was asked the question about the issue of continuity and discontinuity by the Corinthians. Here was his answer. There are different kinds of heavenly bodies—sun, moon, planets, stars.

And these heavenly bodies are clearly different from anything we see on earth. They have a different 'glory': 'There is one glory of the sun, and another glory of the moon, and another glory of the stars; for star differs from star in glory' (1 Cor. 15:41). And then he goes on to provide these contrasts about the present and resurrection body:

The present body is 'natural' but the resurrection body is 'spiritual' (indwelt and suffused by the Holy Spirit rather than any idea of it being non-material).

PRESENT BODY	FUTURE BODY
Perishable	Imperishable
Dishonorable	Honorable
Weak	Powerful

Most telling of all are his words in verse 43: '[The Body] is sown in dishonor; it is raised in glory.' We simply have no idea what these glorious bodies of ours will be capable of in this future existence. I don't know about you, but I can hardly wait!

The supreme blessing of this existence will be the fact that we will be with Christ, not simply for decades or centuries, but forever. That is glory indeed.

Main Point

The new heaven and new earth will be utterly Imagnificent!

Questions for Reflection

- How did this chapter change the way you think about 'heaven' and eternal life with Jesus?
- How does the Bible's vision of the future differ from the rest of the world's?
- Read the last two chapters of Revelation (*Revelation 21-22, the very last chapters in the Bible!*). How does the Bible's teaching about the new heaven and the new earth change the way you live now? How does it offer you hope in your current life situation?

Conclusion: What a Thing of Beauty We Are!

We have covered the entire history from the Garden of Eden to the new heaven and new earth! The truth is, we have barely scratched the surface. There is always more to learn and greater wonders to enjoy. I hope you have begun to appreciate a little more of the dignity of human beings: *who* and *what* you are as someone created by God and one who bears His image. I trust, too, that you are a genuine Christian, one whose expectation for future glory lies in faith alone in Christ alone, not from any works on your part. There is salvation in no other name than Jesus. If you are unsure about this, then I urge you to make yourself right with God immediately. There's not a second to lose.

I also trust that you have a renewed sense of your dignity and value. In Christ, you really are someone very special indeed. You are a child of God and an heir— Christians are 'fellow heirs with Christ, provided we suffer with him in order that we may also be glorified with him' (Rom. 8:17). In a sad world where far too many have no sense of purpose or self-worth, being a Christian and knowing that glory awaits us should give us a tremendous sense of confidence. You have everything to live for!

I hope, too, that you can be someone who brings a little bit of the glory to come into this dark world and fill it with light. As you shine forth the glory of God in your life and interactions with others, *you* are the light of the world (Matt. 5:14). Live every moment of it reflecting the glory of Jesus to those around you. As you enter a room, let your glory-light shine (cf. Phil. 2:15).

We have seen that there is an unbreakable pattern in the work of salvation. What God begins He completes. Having brought you to Jesus and given you a new heart to believe, He intends to bring you all the way home. And you have no conception of the wonders that await you on the other side. Heaven and the new heaven and earth are filled with a beauty that we scarcely glimpsed on this side of the divide. As the hymn-writer puts it, *Glory, Glory dwells in Immanuel's Land.*

Knowing who we are and where we are going is a powerful incentive to grow in grace. Knowing the truth about ourselves, we possess powerful weapons to hurl in Satan's direction and resist him. Knowing that heaven is our home, why should we dabble with sin's pathetic allurements? Knowing that we are God's redeemed children with a ticket to glory, why should we (as Bunyan pictured in his ever-popular *Pilgrim's Progress*) wander into the Castle of Giant Despair?

Heaven awaits and glory in abundance, but until then, God calls us to be joyful, trusting, faithful and confident. We are to live each day glorifying Him and enjoying His presence.

Appendix A: What Now?

- Remind yourself of who you are in Christ. Tell yourself, 'I am a Christian, a child of God, a child of the king, an heir of His promises, indwelt by the Holy Spirit, assured of final victory.'
- Preach the saving and powerful truths of the gospel to yourself every single morning and evening.
- Think about how special you are in Christ. After all, you are loved so much that Jesus died for you. You are an image-bearer. You reflect something of God's glory. In so many ways, you are special.
- Remember that everyone you meet, Christian or not, is an image-bearer of God and deserves respect. The image may be broken, as one Reformer in the sixteenth century put it, like a ruined castle, but its

foundations are still visible. Be dignified and treat others with the same dignity.

- Think about how God's glory might shine into a room you enter, the words you say, the attitude you adopt, the care and respect you convey.
- Remind yourself that you live in two dimensions: you are in this world, but you also sit in 'heavenly places' (Eph. 1:3; 2:6).
- Remember when this world, especially its brokenness, gets you down and robs you of your joy in Christ, that this world is not your home. You have a ticket to heaven in your pocket.
- Spend some time each day thinking about heaven—it's only a breath away! I don't mean this in the sense that you should abandon your calling and responsibilities here in this world. Indeed, it has often been said that people who think about heaven are of no earthly use, but that's a lie. History is full of examples of godly women and men who thought a great deal about heaven and doing so impelled them to improve this world, loving their neighbors in acts of kindness and generosity.

Appendix B: Other Books on this Topic

Tom Barnes, *Living in the Hope of Future Glory: The Glorification of the Christian* (Evangelical Press, 2006).

Anthony A. Hoekema, *The Bible and the Future* (Eerdmans, 1994).

John Murray, *Redemption Accomplished and Applied* (Eerdmans, 2015).

John Piper, *Future Grace: The Purifying Power of the Promises of God* (Multnomah, 2012).

Derek W. H. Thomas, *Heaven on Earth: What the Bible Teaches about Life to Come* (Christian Focus, 2018).

B. B. Warfield, *The Plan of Salvation: The Order of God's Decrees* (Great Christian Books, 2013).

A STUDENT'S GUIDE TO SANCTIFICATION

TRACK

LIGON DUNCAN & JOHN PERRITT

A Student's Guide to Sanctification

LIGON DUNCAN & JOHN PERRITT

Knowing that we have been saved by what Jesus has done rather than by what we have done is amazing. But how does this knowledge affect the way we live? What's the point in being good if we will be forgiven anyway? Actually, the Bible says that God's forgiveness frees us to live for Him, and through the Holy Spirit we can grow to become more and more like Jesus. Ligon Duncan and John Perritt dive into what that means in this short book.

978-1-5271-0451-8

EDWARD T.
WELCH

A Student's Guide to Anxiety

EDWARD T. WELCH

We all know the feeling. That nervous, jittery, tense feeling that tells you that something bad is just ahead. Anxiety can be overwhelming. But the Bible has plenty to say to people who are anxious. This book will help us to take our eyes off our circumstances and fix them on God.

978-1-5271-0450-1

Reformed Youth Ministries (RYM) exists to reach students for Christ and equip them to serve. Passing the faith on to the next generation has been RYM's passion since it began. In 1972 three youth workers who shared a passion for biblical teaching to youth surveyed the landscape of youth ministry conferences. What they found was an emphasis on fun and games, not God's Word. Therefore, they started a conference that focused on the preaching and teaching of God's Word. Over the years RYM has grown beyond conferences into three areas of ministry: conferences, training, and resources.

- **Conferences:** RYM's youth conferences take place in the summer at a variety of locations across the United States and are continuing to expand. We also host parenting conferences throughout the year at local churches.

- **Training:** RYM launched an annual Youth Leader Training (YLT) conference in 2008. YLT has grown steadily through the years and is offered in multiple locations. RYM also offers a Church Internship Program in partnering local churches as well as youth leader coaching and youth ministry consulting.
- **Resources:** RYM offers a variety of resources for leaders, parents, and students. Several Bible studies are offered as free downloads with more titles regularly being added to their catalogue. RYM hosts multiple podcasts: *Parenting Today*, *The Local Youth Worker*, and *The RYM Student Podcast*, all of which can be downloaded on multiple formats. There are many additional ministry tools available for download on the website.

If you are passionate for passing the faith on to the next generation, please visit www.rym.org to learn more about Reformed Youth Ministries. If you are interested in partnering with us in ministry, please visit www.rym.org/donate.

Christian Focus Publications

Our mission statement —

STAYING FAITHFUL

In dependence upon God we seek to impact the world
through literature faithful to His infallible Word, the Bible.
Our aim is to ensure that the Lord Jesus Christ is presented as
the only hope to obtain forgiveness of sin, live a useful life and
look forward to heaven with Him.

Our books are published in four imprints:

CHRISTIAN
FOCUS

Popular works including biographies, commentaries, basic doctrine
and Christian living.

CHRISTIAN
HERITAGE

Books representing some of the
best material from the rich heritage
of the church.

MENTOR

Books written at a level suitable
for Bible College and seminary
students, pastors, and other serious
readers. The imprint includes
commentaries, doctrinal studies,
examination of current issues and
church history.

CF4•K

Children's books for quality Bible
teaching and for all age groups: Sunday
school curriculum, puzzle and activity
books; personal and family devotional
titles, biographies and inspirational sto-
ries — because you are never too young
to know Jesus!

Christian Focus Publications Ltd,
Geanies House, Fearn, Ross-shire,
IV20 1TW, Scotland, United Kingdom.
www.christianfocus.com
blog.christianfocus.com